ALSO BY CARL PHILLIPS

RECONNAISSANCE

FARRAR STRAUS GIROUX   NEW YORK

RECONNAISSANCE

CARL PHILLIPS

FARRAR, STRAUS AND GIROUX
18 WEST 18TH STREET, NEW YORK 10011

PRINTED IN THE UNITED STATES OF AMERICA
FIRST EDITION, 2015

LIBRARY OF CONGRESS CATALOGING-IN-PUBLICATION DATA
PHILLIPS, CARL, 1959–
   [POEMS. SELECTIONS]
   RECONNAISSANCE : POEMS / CARL PHILLIPS — FIRST EDITION.
     PAGES ; CM
    ISBN 978-0-374-24828-4 (HARDCOVER) —
 ISBN 978-0-374-71339-3 (EBOOK)
    I. TITLE.

  PS3566.H476 A6 2015
  811'.54—DC23

                                        2015002966

DESIGNED BY QUEMADURA

FARRAR, STRAUS AND GIROUX BOOKS MAY BE PURCHASED
FOR EDUCATIONAL, BUSINESS, OR PROMOTIONAL USE.
FOR INFORMATION ON BULK PURCHASES, PLEASE CONTACT
THE MACMILLAN CORPORATE AND PREMIUM SALES
DEPARTMENT AT 1-800-221-7945, EXTENSION 5442,
OR WRITE TO SPECIALMARKETS@MACMILLAN.COM.

WWW.FSGBOOKS.COM
WWW.TWITTER.COM/FSGBOOKS
WWW.FACEBOOK.COM/FSGBOOKS

10 9 8 7 6 5 4 3 2 1

TITLE-PAGE ART: TOM KNECHTEL, A VENETIAN HORSE,
1992. PASTEL ON HANDMADE PAPER. NORA ECCLES HARRISON
MUSEUM OF ART, UTAH STATE UNIVERSITY, LOGAN, UTAH,
MARIE ECCLES CAINE FOUNDATION GIFT.

"But most of the time—most of the time I made love only with the body."

"That can make one very lonely," I said. I had not expected to say it.

He had not expected to hear it.

—*JAMES BALDWIN*

CONTENTS

RECONNAISSANCE

RECONNAISSANCE

All the more elegant forms of cruelty, I'm told, begin
with patience. I have practiced patience. As for piety
being, to superstition, as what had seemed a fortress
can be to not-a-fortress-in-the-end, at all: maybe so.

—Why not move like light, reflected, across the snow?

THE DARKER POWERS

Even if you're right,
and there's in fact a difference
between trouble unlooked-for, and
the kind of trouble we pursued,
ruthlessly, until at last
it was ours,

               what will the difference
have been, finally? What I've
called the world continues
to pass for one, the room spins
same as ever, the bodies
inside it do, flightless, but
no less addicted to mastering—
to the dream of mastering—the very
boughs through which
they keep falling without
motion, almost,
that slowly, it seems they'll fall
forever, my

               pretty consorts, to whom
sometimes—out of pity,
not mercy, for
nothing tender

about it—I show the darker
powers I've hardly shown
to anyone: *Feel the weight of them,*
I say, before putting them back,
just behind my heart, where they blacken
and thrive.

FOR NIGHT TO FALL

You could tell from the start that the best

were frailing. We made the wishes we made,
beside the wishes we also hoped would
come true, for there's always a difference,

the way what we remember of what happened
is just memory, not history exactly, and
not the past, which *is* truth, but by then

who cared? The truth by then as a snowy
owl becoming steadily more indistinguishable
from the winter sand in twilight, feathered

emptiness filling/unfilling itself for no one,
no apparent reason—who? who says?
who says the dead are farther away from me

than you are?—across the hard, hard shore.

MORALIA

The Golden Age, the Silver . . . And then there's the nothing
everything returns to, flies to a bloated stag found
strangled, say, among the reeds,

                          the reeds where the roseate,
the thick in the head but all the lovelier for it, the lion-
muscled, graceful, syphilitic—all the lovers you've
ever had, meaning all the bodies you've variously given
sway to

          or made sway—rise as one before you: not ghostly,
more like perennials you'd forgotten to expect again,
finding their way back into the violence and non-violence
of light, sunlight. They're what the light falls through.

THE GREATEST COLORS
FOR THE EMPTIEST
PARTS OF THE WORLD

Sure, I used to say his name like a truth that, just
by saying it aloud, I could make more true, which
makes no more sense than having called it sorrow,
when it was only the rain making the branches hang
more heavily, so that some of them, sometimes,
even touched the ground . . . I see that now. I can

see how easy it is to confuse estrangement with
what comes before that, what's really just another
form of being lost, having meant to spell out—
wordlessly, handlessly—*I'm falling*, not *Sir,*
I fell. As for emptiness spilling where no one
ever wanted it to, and becoming compassion, as

for how that happens— What if all we do is all we
can do? what if longing, annihilation, regret are all this
life's ever going to be, a little music thrown across and
under it, ghost song from a cricket box when the last
crickets have again gone silent, *now, or be still forever*,
as the gathering crowd, ungathering, slowly backs away?

STEEPLE

Maybe love really does mean the submission of power—
I don't know. Like pears on a branch, a shaking branch,
in sunlight, 4 o'clock sunlight, all the ways we do harm,
or refrain from it, when nothing says we have to . . . Shining,
everyone shining like that, as if reality itself depended
on a nakedness as naked as naked gets; on a faith in each
other as mistaken as mistaken tends to be, though I have
loved the mistake of it—still do; even now—as I love
the sluggishness with which, like sacrifice, like the man
who, having seen, no, having understood himself at last,
turns at first away—has to—the folded black-and-copper
wings of history begin their deep unfolding, the bird itself,
shuddering, lifts up into the half-wind that comes after—
higher—soon desire will resemble most that smaller thing,
late affection, then the memory of it; and then nothing at all.

SINCE YOU ASK

It's as if forgiveness were, in fact, an animal—wild,
like animals, the particular wild of animals that have
lived domesticated their entire lives, when a hand,
a trigger, something small lets go. All I can hear
most nights is the howling, even if, sometimes, sure,
I forget to think about it—if I don't think about it,
the dark's pieces briefly come back together, they
lift as one and, like a swarm of bees, thick, ungainly,
in slow reverse, the dark clears. They say one cloud
must pass eventually, from beneath the other—and
I have learned it must: didn't intimacy mean courtesy,
once, and force mean power? I'll shout the starlings
loose from the pines again. I swim the field—stitches
everywhere, your body everywhere, blue cornflowers.

CAPELLA

I

I miss the sea.

I miss the storms
that stopped there.

How much is luck, again opening,
and luck shutting itself down, what we
never expected, or only sort of did,
or should have?

The windfalls of my mistakes sweetly rot beneath me.

Two hawks lift—headed north—from my highest bough.

II

So he's seen the blizzard that the future
looks like, and gotten lost,
a little. All the same—

he gathers the honeysuckle in his arms,
as for a lover. Cloud of bees,
of yellow.

His chest, blurring bright with it.

Who's to say brutality's what he'll be wearing,
when he goes?

III

There's a light that estrangement,
more often than not, briefly
leaves behind it.

           Then the dark—blue and damned,
erotic: here, where—done at last
with flashing like
power itself at first, then what power

comes to—the field
lays down its winded swords. —My head;
beside yours.

CHROMATIC BLACK

Of the many things that he used to say to me, there are two
I'm certain of: *You taste like a last less-than-long summer afternoon*
by the shore just before September; and

You're the kind of betrayal, understand, I've been waiting for,
all my life. When did remembering stop meaning
to be lit from within—bodily—

and the mind, briefly flickering
again out—wasn't that forgetting? Somewhere
abandon's still just a word to be turned away from, as from a man

on fire. Remorse, I think,
is not regret. How new, as in full of chance, the nights here
still can seem to be,

if you keep your eyes closed. Here's a lullaby:
"No more bondage, no triumph, either, no more the bluing waves
of shame . . ."

PERMISSION TO SPEAK

And if I be torn?

And if torn means mendable?

And the wayward mission of your body
be a needle's mission, up and through
my own?

      How softly the after comes
loose, unraveling, until it's just
before: bees again in the catnip, the yarrow,
the last of those hydrangeas that I call
forgiveness, for their useless unfolding and
flowering routinely, each time as if
this time something different will be
what happens,

      not the usual ghost of
put-aside-for-now sorrow
disappearing, none of that
steadiness with which
he kept looking back—back at both of us,
as he lifted away.

DISCIPLINE

More theatrically than I'd expected,
the trapped hummingbird won't stop
beating the mason jar's glass.

The staghorn sumac's
splayed geometry
tilts on the wind.

You are the knife,
and you are also what the knife
has opened, says the wind.

FOR LONG TO HOLD

Not because there was nothing to say, or we
didn't want to—we just stopped speaking
entirely, but like making a gift of it: *Here;*
      for you. Saturday birds picked the sidewalk's
reminders of Friday night's losses, what got left
behind. I've been wrong about more than, despite
      memory, I had thought was possible. I keep
making my way through the so-called forests of the so-
called dead, I whistle their branches into rivers
      elsewhere, they tell the usual lies that water, lately,
can hardly wait to begin singing about: love as
rescue, rescue as to have been at last set free. If
      that's how it always seems anyway, so what,
that it did? When I whistle again—not so hard
this time, more softly—each lie blows out, then
      away: lit candles; dust. —I take everything back.

STAMINA

     —Wild West? Colorless birds
lift up from the snarl and
tangle of chaparral. Twice
     I've known the speed of love
to exactly equal the speed of
life itself. Not so much
     the saguaro's predictability,
but the more ignorable
vegetation. All the smaller
     varieties of almost that, before
living without them, we thought
we'd die without. In these parts,
     reptilian, autoerotic, that's
how the winter works, when it
comes, if it does come. I keep
     a space for tenderness. The Wild
West isn't dead yet, it seems,
no; only harder to find. Is it
     any wonder—were we not
a wonder—seeing how the skies here,
how they give everything away too soon?

THE LENGTH OF THE FIELD

In the stories it's different: grief,
like the dark, lifts eventually—
an abandonment inside which, with all
the clarity of bells when for once they
ring like nothing but the ringing bells
they are, it can seem that at last you've

gotten away with something, like
a horse you've stolen that, now, lighter
than ash on a sudden wind, or any wind
at all, takes the length of the field, but
as if bewildered almost, any man
for whom to have trusted too easily

has merely meant disappointment,
not disaster, and the long
longing-in-vain for that moment when
either one could have been the other
starts to stir a little, slowly it unfurls itself,
its languorous disease, inside him.

THE BURIED LIFE

Crazy week. Highlights include—not by
coincidence, it seems—two men offering me
their different versions of whatever marriage can
even mean, at this point—the one bringing me
three varieties of oranges, to test for sweetness,
the other not . . . Sometimes I wake to my own
voice saying again—but to whom?—*If I
believed in forgiveness, here's what I'd say to you,
I shall never forgive myself.* I can't think
what I might have done, that I should have to
say such a thing, and yet I know myself
better than that. Therefore, what have I done?

*

Just the way it's always been: first the word for
twilight, then the word for deer light. The meadow
darkens in the wake of another year's only Full
Thunder Moon. All of it done, now. The years reduce
to a gone-to-rags-at-last chorus of blinded messengers
dwindling fast behind me, like what remains of love,
the parts about it still worth understanding, I mean,
not the parts that aren't. How much later it is,
than I'd ever thought to hope for. Whether
he was generous, or just resourceful, I'll never know.

AFTER LEARNING THAT THE
SPELL IS IRREVERSIBLE

In the fresco of you telling me the dream
all over again—one dog killing another,
the larger one taking the smaller one's
head in its mouth, and biting down, waiting
for that stillness that,

                sometimes, I don't
feel anymore like waiting for—how cold
it is; how windless. Did you know there
are animals that will spend their entire
lives in silence, if they don't get killed

by something more violent, more alive
somehow? I used to think it was as if fear,
or panic, had brought into voice, finally,
whatever scrap of sound they'd always
held inside them,

              but lately I wonder:
Was it there from the start, or does it come
from elsewhere, gift-like,

                like a kind of
song to at least go down singing? Hard
to believe there was nothing I wouldn't
have done for you—harder still, that I ever

said so. In the dream, the surviving dog
keeps changing colors—courage and shame,
rage,

      devotion—as he disappears into
a field that, in turn, keeps changing: now a field;
now life as it might have been; now the sea,
whose history—like its signature—is ruin.

FROM A LAND CALLED NEAR-IS-FAR

But what if all suffering is in fact for nothing—
no particular wisdom after, blooming flower-like,
blood in the water? To be stripped of one's armor
and left naked, dying, on a field of war—that's what
humiliation meant, once. Remember? There's a color
I've seen, sometimes, just before some larger mistake
happens that will change everything, and forever,
soon a life will turn—even now, begins to . . . Mercy's
a cliff, I think; a sea adorns it; if I forget the name, if
I forget what I called the sea—here, beneath the several
whips of the smoke tree's twisted branches—what's
it matter? How at bay the light seems. For once, let's
be still. Together. It could be hunger, it could be sex,
that smell, or fearfulness, or just fear by itself—tenderer
hands than ours, soundlessly, as they at last unyoke us.

CORRECTION

Look closer, he said.

I saw a scattering of arrowheads, easily
missed at first, above which the river, unspooling,
unspooled itself with all the generosity
of a mirror, water's cool, see-throughable
commitment . . . All of this

inside his dying body, from which I turned,
as I believe he wanted me to, like a
well-trained horse that, startled
suddenly, then remembering somehow a way

through panic, begins again ascending,
ceremonial almost, now
renegotiates the more

difficult branches, where they fell, kept falling . . .

SPIRIT LAKE

All the several darknesses that I hated once,
though more often, lately, I row inside them,
stolen boats, blown aslant these waters . . .

—Gracchus, fallen hunter, in your boat called
Little Crown, O crown of Death, I don't
forget you. Even now, I trespass in your name.

IN WHICH TO WONDER FLEW
A KIND OF RECKONING

So turned our backs to where woundable
had come to mean therefore wounded. Stepped
past bravery's blurred, curtains-in-a-wind
façade. A birdlessness, and yet, from the trees
everywhere, the smallest sounds . . . As when,
for example, the by-now-nearly-ritualized
mistake of falling self-destructively
and in relatively slow motion into then
out of love seems to stop, a moment,
all the slaughtered chances we convinced
ourselves a life equaled, they suddenly fit
in one hand, our mistakes mean nothing, the field
lies down—it stammers in flames, before us . . .

LOWISH HUM, COOL FUSS

Like hawks tipping, fluttering, over likely ruin—
how what looks to be patience isn't patience
at all, more like hunger and instinct squaring
off before joining forces, late sun, soon the night,
soon enough the kill—I've been, as best as
I can, honest. I can talk about longing, sure,
or I can change

                  the subject. They say innocence
is a kind of insanity, for example—let it fail, as it
should, as it has to . . . But why can't innocence
be instead a boat, slowly coming about, set free
by accident, beneath it the rocks against which
sturdier craft, I know, have shattered? I've done myth—
history's easy. I came a long way, sir, to reach you.

LAST NIGHT

Then he said it was like learning
the hard way—as in, too late—
that maybe recklessness
        is overrated, and though I disagreed,
I did not say so. I disembarked
instead . . . Behind me, the skiff
        keeps nudging the pier, rough
sex diminishing or just now
revealing itself—a distinction that,
        from here, I can see
matters; it should. It should have.
Sometimes the light can seem
        to stand in for reluctance—
last night, the dark did. I have rested
my hand on the beloved's head. As with
        regret—so, too, with prayer. His
skull; my hand. There's
a trembling inside the both of us,
        there's a trembling, inside us both.

FOLIAGE

Cage inside a cage inside a whispering so deep that
—And then just the two of us. And you calling it
vulnerability. And me calling it rumor passing
through suspicion's fingers—ashweed, flickering
halo of the boy I might really have been once, tiger
lilies beneath a storm blowing into then out of
character, then back again, as if seasonal, summer
now, now fall. But I know suspicion has no fingers.
Vulnerability's just part of the trash that rumor leaves
behind. Wait it out long enough, the trash shifts, it
always does, in that way it's like memory lately—
I'm the fist of instinct, cool, unstoppable, you're
the dogwood's crucifix-laden branches, I'm the fist
through the branches, you're the fist, I'm the branches . . .

THE STRONG BY THEIR STILLNESS

Most mornings here, mist is the first thing to go—first
the mist, then the fog, though hardly anyone seems to know
the difference, or even care, the way for some a dead buck
is a dead buck: the road, the body, a little light, the usual
dark, light's

              unshakeable escort . . . You can love a man
more than he'll ever love back or be able to, you can confuse
your understanding of that

                         with a thing like acceptance or,
worse, all you've ever deserved. I've driven hard into
the gorgeousness of spring before; it fell hard behind me:
the turning away, I mean, the finding of clothes,
the maneuvering

              awkwardly back into them . . . why not drive
forever? Respect or shame, it's pretty much your
own choice, is how it once got explained to me. I've already
said—I'm not sorry. Magnolia. Wild pear. So what if one
wish begets a next one,

                   only to be conquered by it, if the blooms
break open nevertheless like hope?

THUNDER

Maybe not ourselves, for once, but each other

*

Not the wilder doves;
not their blurred machinery leaving the less wild doves behind

FAINTLY, WITH FALLING STARS

Like having been lost unfindably, and then
not so much remembering the way, as the way
itself somehow opening: *Watch me*. And you
understanding at last—not just knowing it—
the difference, for there

                      is a difference, power
being one thing, survival another. If he
never believed you did, can you really say
you loved him, and what you say be true?

At the water's edge—as at the edge of ruin,
the kind that's meant to be looked back on once,
then it's gone, forgotten—you lift two fingers.
Your eyes shift eastward. Conquest. And,
by whatever name, the glittering

                          slaves that
always follow conquest, like a bridal train. How
flushed the bride looks, pulling your broken face
—not untenderly—toward hers, less broken.

DELICATELY, SLOW,
THE WORLD COMES BACK

Usefulness, thin as figment, but sturdier,
sturdy enough, may well end up the one gift I've
been able to give, that I didn't take back. So? The bamboo

does its folding and unfolding thing anyway, under the wind,
across, over it. Hard to say how the parts that hurt in life,
most of them, ever come to pass. The wild dog in my head

that I keep for company, that I'd been told could
not be tamed, which is why I wanted him, I think,
or I think so now, becomes daily more tractable: I raise

my hand; he fairly falls beneath it. Half of me says I'm
the wrong answer, while the other says no, maybe
just more difficult, the harder one

to choose. The dog looks up at me,
then quickly away. Pretty soon, I'll have broken him. Little prize;
bit of trophy. —And what will usefulness be then?

ENOUGH, TOM FOOL, NOW SLEEP

It's as if the sea could listen, could be listening
now, though that's impossible; I know. Like
certain faces, their way of blurring at once
ceremonial, flat, civilian—then they clear,
skies beneath which the leaves spiraled like what
looked like forever, mapling even the steeper

shafts in memory, parts the light all but missed,
keeps missing . . . Husbandry turns out to have been,
if hard, then not the hardest thing: I can care; I've
cared. If never quite rescue—nowhere near as
blue as that—then at least reprieve, whispering

What the heavenly fuck are those tears for? Lately
that, too, seems impossible. I don't see any tears.
What I see: a fox paw for a paperweight; the 19th
century as random taxidermied sparrow—domed
in glass, mid-flight . . . Maybe not the wings, this time;
not the underwings, either. Dare me to stay. I'll stay.

MEANWHILE, AND ANYWAY

Otherwise, what of empathy,
or any way to get there: upriver,
and then what? Leaves, or
    the burst and fall of them,
or just the stripped-by-now
branches—comes to all
    the same: false witness,
a smell like licorice, stolen
seawater as it begins to turn,
    whatever boy stumbles
lost inside the man
flickering almost back, chance
    when it still lies smoldering,
but nowhere a wind yet,
nothing stirs, everything
    could happen . . . Easily,
lazily, I sway. You were right,
I think; I was wrong:
    acceptance as the too-long-
missing counterweight
to the staggered weightlessness
    of sorrow, regret—the old

angers, too? Why not? Ravens,
horses; another barn on fire—
        it used to feel that lonely.
Impenetrable, the logic
by which I mistook your hand
        in the night, last night, for mine.

HARNESS

As for Risk: I've held
on to him. And yes—
I still ride, though he
        moves more slowly now,
with something a bit like
the grace that, over time,
        promiscuity can seem
to bring with it, or—if we're
lucky enough—defeat,
        after. He's older, of course;
we're all older . . . Do you
remember predicting—
        even hoping, maybe—
that I would be lonely here, and
regret my decision? Lay it
        down. How almost blue
he looks against the sand tonight,
in this light—crippled
        light; light that's leaving.

SHIELD

Like the restoration of order
     to a shambled kingdom, there are things
in the end that shouldn't last—aren't at
     least supposed to . . . If briefly I've cast
the world, though, as a place you almost
     believed in enough to stay—stay
inside of—I say it counts as magic: wind coming
     shoreward, night coming down
all over again, lone Atlas moth hanging, providing
     color to its patch of shade, where it mates,
then dies, not so much victoriousness
     as victory, even if a restless one—if I've
been restless, then the way a compass can be,
     and still be true.

AT BAY

Coral bells purpled the fallen sycamore leaves, dead, the dead
versus those who attempted death, versus those who effectively
fashioned out of such attempts a style akin to electric guitar
shimmer swelling and unswelling like starlings when they first

lift off, or like stars when, from their fixed sway, they come
suddenly loose, the hero lets go—all gone, a career spent
swallowing, trying to, catastrophe's jewel-studded tail, un-
swallowable, because

                    holy, in the way of fanfare, its gift for
persuasion, how it can make of what's ordinary, and therefore
flawed of course, a thing that's holy, for a time it seemed so,
didn't restlessness seem to be, little god of making, no less

impossible in the end than any of the gods, where's the holiness,
they sleep never, they tire infrequently, to be tired bores them,
distraction refined by damage would be their drug of choice
hands down, if they could choose, even they don't get to.

SPRING

Pointing first to the rock bluffs, then the raptors that
hovered there, and then to their eyes that—made for
hunting—flashed like shattered quartz, pulled up wild
from the sea, the fog having lifted, hours, centuries ago,
Choose one, he said,

                whispering almost; *Choose quickly*.
As between forever, and the light now fallen. The willed
suspension of belief, say, versus the color of joy outrivaling
whoever's best intentions. That's how hard it was. Any words
left that had stood for something

                      still meaning, but in the way
that moss can mean: all winter; beneath the ice and snow.

BY FORCE

Look—they're turning: how gracefully each
    moves, in the surprise of woundedness—and,
where arrow meets flesh, the blood corsaging . . .

    Revelation, jackhammers, love, four hooves
in the dirt. How speechless, now. As if always
    light must wed the dark, eventually, and the dark

mean silence. I disagree. Touch not the crown— Don't touch me—

ACKNOWLEDGMENTS

Many thanks to the editors of the journals in which these poems, some in different form, initially appeared:

Academy of American Poets: "At Bay"
The Cincinnati Review: "Since You Ask" (as "Hold Tight")
Fogged Clarity: "Reconnaissance," "Thunder"
Gulf Coast: "Enough, Tom Fool, Now Sleep"
Harvard Review: "Delicately, Slow, the World Comes Back"
Iron Horse Literary Review: "Lowish Hum, Cool Fuss"
The Journal: "Moralia"
The Kenyon Review: "Capella," "In Which to Wonder Flew a Kind of Reckoning," "Last Night," "Meanwhile, and Anyway," "Stamina"
Literary Imagination: "Faintly, with Falling Stars"
Little Star: "Foliage," "From a Land Called Near-Is-Far"
Martha's Vineyard Arts & Ideas: "After Learning That the Spell Is Irreversible"
The Massachusetts Review: "Correction," "The Darker Powers"
Nat. Brut: "Permission to Speak," "Spirit Lake"
New England Review: "By Force," "Spring"
The New Republic: "Harness," "Steeple"
The Paris-American: "The Greatest Colors for the Emptiest Parts of the World" (as "In This Light")
The Pinch: "The Buried Life"
Ploughshares: "Chromatic Black," "The Length of the Field"
Plume: "For Night to Fall"

Washington Square: "Discipline," "Shield" (as "Each Like a Branch
   Thrown Slant Across")
The Yale Review: "For Long to Hold," "The Strong by Their Stillness"

The epigraph is from James Baldwin's *Giovanni's Room* (New York:
Vintage, 2013).

"The Greatest Colors for the Emptiest Parts of the World": The title
is from the last two lines of "Octavia," by Tim Dlugos, from *Strong
Place* (New York: Amethyst Press, 1992).

"Steeple": The opening sentence responds to an assertion by Gillian
Rose in *Love's Work* (New York: New York Review Books, 2011).

"For Long to Hold": The title is from Hart Crane's "The Broken
Tower," in *Complete Poems of Hart Crane*, ed. Marc Simon (New York:
Liveright, 1993).

"Spirit Lake": Gracchus here refers to the hunter in Franz Kafka's
short story "The Hunter Gracchus," with which this poem is in
conversation. Cf. *The Complete Stories*, trans. Nahum Norbert Glatzer
(New York: Shocken Books, 1971).

"Lowish Hum, Cool Fuss": The idea of innocence as a kind of
insanity comes from Graham Greene's *The Quiet American* (New York:
Penguin, 2004).

"The Strong by Their Stillness": The title comes from a sentence in
Juan Pablo Villalobos's *Down the Rabbit Hole*, trans. Rosalind Harvey
(New York: Farrar, Straus and Giroux, 2012).